FREEDOM IN CHRIST

THE STEPS TO FREEDOM IN CHRIST FOR TEENS

Expanded and updated from *The Steps to Freedom in Christ for Young Adults*
© 2009 by Neil T Anderson
Revisions and updates added by Chris Campbell, Rich Miller and Dave Park

Published by Freedom in Christ Ministries
9051 Executive Park Dr., Suite 503
Knoxville, TN 37923
www.ficm.org

ISBN 9780996972529 (pbk)
ISBN 9780996972543 (eBook)

All rights reserved. No part of this book may be reproduced or transmitted in any form or by any means, electronic or mechanical, including photocopying, recording or by any information storage and retrieval system, without permission of the authors or publisher, except for the inclusion of a brief quotation in a review or article, when credit to the book, publisher and order information are included in the review or article.

© 2021 Freedom in Christ.

Scripture quotations marked ESV are taken from The ESV® Bible (The Holy Bible, English Standard Version®), copyright © 2001 by Crossway, a publishing ministry of Good News Publishers. Used by permission. All rights reserved.

Scripture quotations marked NIV are taken from The Holy Bible, New International Version® NIV® Copyright © 1973 1978 1984 2011 by Biblica, Inc. TM. Used by permission. All rights reserved worldwide.

Scripture quotations marked NLT are taken from the Holy Bible, New Living Translation, copyright ©1996, 2004, 2015 by Tyndale House Foundation. Used by permission of Tyndale House Publishers, Carol Stream, Illinois 60188. All rights reserved.

Cover design and layout by Courtney Pierce Design Co. (courtneypierce.net)

Knoxville, Tennessee

Printed in the United States of America

PREFACE

God wants you to be free! It is our deep belief that the finished work of Jesus Christ and the presence of God in our lives are the only means by which we can break free from our personal and spiritual problems. Christ in us is our single hope (Col. 1:27), and He alone can meet our deepest needs of life: acceptance, identity, security, and significance. *The Steps to Freedom in Christ* is not a self-help workbook. *The Steps to Freedom in Christ* is a guided prayer encounter with the God of the Bible. He is the Wonderful Counselor. He is the One who can reveal to your mind every burden and sin that holds you back from experiencing victory and breakthrough (Hebrews 12:1). It is God alone who can unload the heaviness of your soul by forgiving and cleansing you from sin (1 John 1:9).

The Steps to Freedom in Christ do not set you free. **Who** sets you free is Jesus Christ, and **what** sets you free is the way you respond to Him through obedience and faith. *The Steps to Freedom in Christ* is a biblically based, time-tested guide to help you align your free will (choice) with God's grace and truth. *The Steps to Freedom in Christ* will also guide you into a correct way to resist the negative spiritual forces in your life that desire you to fail. As James 4:7 instructs, we are to submit to God and resist the Devil, then he will flee.

Pay careful attention to the words that come before and after James 4:7:

> But he [God] gives more grace. Therefore it says, "God opposes
> the proud but gives grace to the humble." Submit yourselves
> therefore to God. Resist the Devil, and he will flee from you.
> Draw near to God, and he will draw near to you....
> JAMES 4:6-8A ESV

It takes humility to admit your flaws and the wrong you've committed. To be free in Christ and walk in victory, you need to be willing to deal with the things deep in your heart that cause you the most shame. The verses above provide assurance that when you humble yourself in honesty before God, you are given **more** grace. Grace is God's unmistakable favor. Notice that the way to secure God's grace is not to clean up your life first. Instead, you are invited to draw near to God in your imperfection. And by grace, God will draw near to you. This is not an invitation to get the back of God's hand in judgment. This is not an invitation to a stern lecture about your faults and mistakes. Rather, this is an invitation to forgiveness, cleansing and healing while driving away the Devil himself and any other lesser, dark spiritual agents that may be harassing you with temptation, shame or finger-pointing (accusation and condemnation). Wow! God is so good.

Although some teens can work through these steps on their own, we advise you to reach out for help and guidance; specifically, help that comes in the form of a Freedom in Christ Encourager and a prayer partner. They can give you instruction, encouragement, and prayer support. More important than that, God's word speaks to the blessing of confessing our sins in the presence of other people. Confessing our sins to each other brings a new level of forgiveness and healing (James 5:13-16), and walking in the light produces a deeper connection with others (1 John 1:7). When we experience the grace and love of another person in the face of our worst sins, we have a physical and tangible experience of God's gracious love toward us. Teens throughout the world endorse this approach and testify to the blessing of having another physical person in the room who is a real-time, audible mouthpiece of God's grace and love.

As you, by faith, complete each step, the wonderful freedom that Jesus Christ purchased for you on the cross will be secured. And along with this, the peace of God, which surpasses all understanding, will guard your heart and mind (Phil. 4:7). This truth is especially important because there is a battle that takes place in the mind of every person who desires to be free in Christ. You may be tempted to think that your struggle is too great, your shame is too enormous or Satan's control over you is too powerful, but none of these are true when you humbly come to God and seek freedom (James 4:6-8a). Remember, the God who loves you and saves you by the sacrifice of Jesus Christ is all-powerful, always present, and all-knowing. He is willing and able to deliver you. God is always greater by a long shot.

While working through *The Steps*, you may experience nagging thoughts like "This isn't going to work" or "God doesn't love me" or "What if I'm not serious enough?" These thoughts are lies and distractions. If these lies are quietly considered, you will struggle to work through the steps. Therefore, commit yourself to the following strategy:

FOR THE TEEN PARTICIPANT: You must cooperate with the person who is trying to help you. Do this by openly sharing what is going on inside your mind. Let this person know when you are experiencing doubt and opposing thoughts. Be direct about the thoughts.

Also, if you experience any physical discomfort (e.g., headache, nausea, tightness in the throat, etc.), don't be alarmed. Just tell the person you are with so he/she can pray for you and encourage you.

So...let's do this!

As believers in Christ, we can pray with authority to stop any interference by Satan. All prayers and declarations throughout *The Steps* should be **read aloud**. Below is a prayer and declaration to get you started. It is to be spoken aloud by the encourager who is assisting you. You can also pray this prayer aloud for yourself.

OPENING PRAYER

Dear Heavenly Father, we know that You are currently here in this room with us and that You are present in our lives right now. You are the only all-knowing, all-powerful, and ever-present God. We are completely dependent upon You because without Jesus Christ we can do nothing. We choose to stand in the truth of Your Word, and we refuse to believe the Devil's lies. We thank You that the risen Lord Jesus has all authority in heaven and on earth. Father, because we are in Christ, we share His authority to make disciples and set captives free. We ask You to protect our minds and bodies during this time. Please fill us with the Holy Spirit so that He can guide us into all truth. We choose to follow His guidance alone during this time. Please reveal to our minds everything that You want us to deal with today. We ask for and trust in Your wisdom. We pray all this in faith, in the name of Jesus. Amen.

DECLARATION

In the name and authority of the Lord Jesus Christ, we command any and all evil spiritual agents to release their hold on _____(name)_____ in order that _____(name)_____ can be free to know and choose to do the will of God. As children of God, raised up and given a position in Heaven with Jesus, we agree that every enemy of the Lord Jesus Christ be bound and silenced. We say to Satan and all his evil workers that you cannot inflict any distress or in any way prevent God's will from being done today in _____(name)_____ life.

There are seven steps to help you claim your rightful freedom in Christ. You will cover the areas where the world, the flesh and the Devil most often take advantage of humans and where strongholds of the mind are commonly built. Jesus Christ purchased your victory when He shed His blood for you on the cross. You will experience your freedom when you make the choice to *believe, confess, forgive, renounce,* and *forsake*. No one can do this for you. The battle for your mind can only be won as you *personally* choose to act upon the truth in simple obedience and humility.

As you go through *The Steps to Freedom in Christ*, remember that even Satan is not powerful enough to read your mind. Thus, he won't obey your thoughts. Only God knows what you are thinking. Therefore, as you go through each step, it is important that you submit to God inwardly and resist the Devil by reading **aloud** each prayer—*verbally* renouncing, forgiving, confessing, etc.

With the Holy Spirit's guidance, you are going to be taking a thorough look at your life in order to get drastically right with God. If it turns out that you have another kind of problem (not covered in these steps) which is negatively affecting your life, you will have lost nothing. If you are open and honest during this time, you will greatly benefit by becoming right with God and close to Him.

May the Lord greatly bless you and touch your life during this time. He will give you the strength to make it through. It is essential that you work through *all* seven steps, so don't allow yourself to become discouraged and give up. Remember, the freedom that Christ purchased for all believers on the cross is meant for *you!*

STEP 1: COUNTERFEIT VS. REAL

The first step toward experiencing your freedom in Christ is to *renounce*—to vocally reject and turn away from—all past, present and future involvement in satanic inspired occult practices, non-Christian religions or things done in secret.

Here is a simple definition for you to consider:

OCCULT PRACTICES—The individual or group pursuit of supernatural, mystical, or magical beliefs, practices, or phenomena that God has plainly forbidden in the Bible.

The first step toward your freedom involves confessing, repenting and renouncing any occult group or practices that you've been exposed to or participated in. Specifically, to be free, you need to renounce any activity and group that denies Jesus Christ is Lord, offers direction through any source other than the Word of God (the Holy Bible), encourages immorality, or requires secret initiations, ceremonies, promises or pacts (ungodly vows). Begin this important step with the following prayer:

LET'S PRAY

> Dear Heavenly Father, I ask You to guard my heart and my mind and to reveal to me anything that I have done or has been done to me which is spiritually wrong. Reveal to my mind any and all involvement I have knowingly or unknowingly had with cult or occult practices, false teachers and ungodly virtual activities. I ask this in Jesus' name. Amen.

Even if you took part in something as a game or as a joke, you need to renounce it. Satan will try to take advantage of anything he can in our lives. Even if you just stood by and watched others do it, you need to renounce it. Even if you did it just once and had no idea it was evil, you still need to renounce it. You want to remove any and every possible foothold of Satan in your life.

NON-CHRISTIAN SPIRITUAL EXPERIENCES CHECK LIST

(Please check all those that apply to you)

FEAR-BASED/OCCULT SLEEPOVER GAMES:

- ◯ Sweet Tooth
- ◯ Table Lifting or Body Lifting (Light as a Feather)
- ◯ Bloody Mary
- ◯ Ouija Board
- ◯ Sandman
- ◯ Baby Blue
- ◯ The Answer Man
- ◯ Sinking into the Carpet
- ◯ Magic Eight Ball
- ◯ Other

GATEWAYS TO COUNTERFEIT/ SPIRITUALLY ENSLAVING EXPERIENCES:

- ◯ Practicing out of body experiences
- ◯ Using Spells or curses
- ◯ Chants/Mantras
- ◯ Mental Control of Others
- ◯ Automatic Writing
- ◯ Spirit Guides
- ◯ Fortune Telling/Tarot cards
- ◯ Palm Reading/Tea Leaves
- ◯ Astrology/Horoscopes
- ◯ Hypnosis
- ◯ Séances
- ◯ Black or White Magic
- ◯ Dungeons and Dragons (Or other fantasy role-playing games that pulls the mind into magical and/or violent practices that the Bible forbids.)
- ◯ Video or computer games involving occult powers or cruel violence
- ◯ Cutting yourself or harming yourself on purpose
- ◯ Objects of worship/good luck charms
- ◯ Superstitions
- ◯ Trying to connect sexually with the spirit world
- ◯ Seeking healing through New Age Medicine or Alternative Practices that require giving yourself over to supernatural forces other than the God of the Bible (Crystals, Shamans, folklore superstitions).

SECRET SOCIETIES AND CLUBS:

- ◯ Gang membership
- ◯ Making Blood pacts
- ◯ Free Mason Youth Groups/Rainbow Girls
- ◯ Secret societies tied to private schools and universities that involve deviant vows, initiation rituals and activities that are biblically immoral/forbidden

FALSE RELIGIONS: *(Groups and practices that deny the identity of Jesus Christ as Savior and Lord and the exclusive authority of the Holy Bible.)*

- ○ Mormonism
- ○ Jehovah Witnesses
- ○ Scientology
- ○ Islam
- ○ Buddhism
- ○ Hinduism
- ○ Making Idols of rock stars, actors/actresses, sports heroes, etc. (People who surpass the God of the Bible in holding your attention, time, resources and affection.)

For a list of more false religions that you might have been exposed to, check out the expanded list in **Appendix C**.

Other experiences that are coming to mind now: _____

_____

_____

_____

_____

_____

_____

NOTE: This is not a complete list. If you have any doubts about an activity not included here, renounce your involvement in it. If it has come to mind here, trust that the Lord wants you to renounce it.

Let's think about entertainment you've been exposed to that outwardly defied God's values and the way of Jesus. List below those things that especially glorified Satan or sinful behavior, caused fear or nightmares, or were gruesomely violent.

ANTI-CHRISTIAN MOVIES:

_____

_____

_____

ANTI-CHRISTIAN MUSIC:

_____

_____

_____

ANTI-CHRISTIAN TV SHOWS:

_____

_____

_____

Once you have completed your list, confess and renounce each item you were involved in by praying aloud the following prayer. Repeat the prayer separately for each item on your list.

LET'S PRAY

Lord, I confess that I have participated in _____. I renounce any and all influence and involvement with _____ and thank you that in Christ I am forgiven.

COUNTERFEIT EXPERIENCES

It's hard, if not impossible, to deny experiences that are other-worldly and/or spiritual in nature. Therefore, we need to acknowledge all spiritual experiences and use the wisdom of the Bible to understand that not every spirit that comes to us is from God. Some may be evil and deceptive in nature (1 John 4:1-4).

- ○ Have you ever heard, seen or felt an evil spiritual presence in your room or somewhere else?

- ○ Do you currently have or have you had an imaginary friend, spirit guide or angel offering you guidance and companionship?

- ○ Have you ever heard voices in your head or had repeating negative, nagging thoughts such as "I'm dumb," "I'm ugly," "Nobody loves me," "I can't do anything right," etc. as if a conversation was going on in your head? Explain.

- ○ Have you ever consulted a palm reader, medium, spiritist, or someone claiming to be a channel for a dead person's spirit to enter and speak to you?

- ○ What other spiritual experiences have you had that would be considered out of the ordinary (knowing something supernaturally, special spiritual gifts, contact with aliens, etc.)?

- ○ Have you ever been involved in satanic worship of any kind or attended a concert at which Satan was the focus?

- ○ Do you experience a reoccurring nightmare(s) that leaves you scared and confused?

- ○ Have you ever made an unholy vow or promise? *Note: Not all vows are bad. For example, a marriage vow between a man and woman is a good thing. However, many young people make personal vows in moments of pain that influence the course of life and impair cooperation with God. Examples of unwise vows would be as follows: "I'll never marry;" "I will never be poor;" "I will not live beyond 30 years;" etc.*

Again, once you have completed the above checklist, confess and renounce each counterfeit experience you were involved in by praying aloud the following prayer. Make sure to repeat the prayer separately for each checked experience.

LET'S PRAY

Lord, I confess that I have experienced _____.
I renounce any and all influence and involvement with this counterfeit experience.
Thank you that in Christ, I am forgiven and free.

Unfortunately, a significant number of young people have been exposed to forms of satanic rituals. If you or the individual going through *The Steps to Freedom* has been involved in any Satanic ritual or heavy occult activity (or you suspect it because of blocked memories, severe and recurring nightmares or severe sexual bondage), you will need to say out loud the special renunciations and affirmations in **Appendix C** in the back of this book.

STEP 2: DECEPTION VS. TRUTH

God's Word is true, and we need to accept the truth deep in our hearts (Psalm 51:6). What God says is true whether we feel like it is true or not.

Jesus is the truth (John 14:6), the Holy Spirit is the Spirit of truth (John 16:13), and the Word of God is truth (John 17:11). We ought to speak the truth in love (Ephesians 4:15). The believer in Christ has no business deceiving others by lying, exaggerating, telling little lies, or stretching the truth. Satan is the father of lies (John 8:44), and he seeks to keep people in bondage through deception (Revelation 12:9; 2 Timothy 2:26). But it is the truth in Jesus that sets us free (John 8:32-36). Think about this: by definition, a person who is deceived is unaware of the lie that is influencing him. We need the truth to expose any lies that exist in our minds.

We will find real joy and freedom when we stop living a lie and walk openly in the truth. After confessing his sin, King David concluded that there is great blessing for the person in whose spirit there is no dishonesty (Psalm 32:2).

How can we find the strength to walk in the light of truth (1 John 1:7-9)? When we are sure that God loves and accepts us, we can be free to own up to our sin, face reality and not run or hide from painful experiences.

Start this step by praying the following prayer aloud. Don't let any opposing thoughts such as, "This is a waste of time" or "I wish I could believe this stuff, but I just can't" keep you from praying and choosing the truth. Belief is a choice. If you choose to believe what you feel, then Satan, the "father of lies," will keep you in bondage. You must choose to believe what God says, regardless of what your feelings might say. Even if you have a hard time doing so, pray the following prayer:

LET'S PRAY

Dear Heavenly Father, I know that You want me to know the truth, believe the truth, speak the truth and live in accordance with the truth. Thank You that it is the truth that will set me free. I suspect that I have been deceived by Satan, the father of lies, and I have probably deceived myself as well. Father, I pray in the name of the Lord Jesus Christ, by virtue of His shed blood and resurrection, that You would rebuke all of Satan's demons that are deceiving me. I trust in Jesus alone to save me, and so I am Your forgiven and favored child. Therefore, since You accept me, I can be free to face my sin and not try to hide. I ask the Holy Spirit to guide me into all truth. I ask you to "search me, O God, and know my heart; test me and know my anxious thoughts. See if there is any offensive way in me, and lead me in the way everlasting" (Psalm 139:23-24 NIV). In the name of Jesus, Who is the Truth, I pray. Amen.

There are many ways in which Satan, "the god of this world" (2 Corinthians. 4:4), seeks to deceive us. Just as he did with Eve, the devil tries to convince us to rely on ourselves and get our needs met through the world around us, rather than trusting in our Father in heaven.

The following exercise will help open your eyes to the ways you have been deceived by the world systems around you. Check each area of deception that the Lord confirms in your mind and confess it, using the prayer following the list.

WAYS YOU CAN BE DECEIVED BY THE WORLD:

- ◯ Believing that collecting money and possessions will bring lasting happiness (Matthew 13:22; 1 Timothy 6:10)

- ◯ Believing that using alcohol, forms of tobacco or drugs (including marijuana) will control my pain and increase my happiness (Proverbs 20:1)

- ◯ Believing that my relationship with food (overeating to feel "full"; binging and purging to feel relief; under eating to feel in control) can help me feel real satisfaction (Proverbs 23:19-21)

- ◯ Believing that a sexy, attractive body and a flirtatious personality will get me whatever I want or need (Proverbs 31:10; 1 Peter 3:3-4)

- ◯ Believing that pleasing sexual lust will bring lasting pleasure (Ephesians 4:22; 1 Peter 2:11)

- ◯ Believing that I can secretly sin and it won't affect my heart and character (Hebrews 3:12, 13)

- ◯ Believing that God cannot be totally trusted to take care of my needs (2 Corinthians 11:2-4, 13-15)

- ◯ Believing that because of my personal hardship, I am entitled/allowed to do whatever I want (Obadiah 1:3; 1 Peter 5:5)

- ◯ Believing that I am important and strong and that no one can really be in charge of me (Proverbs 16:18)

- ◯ Believing that people can ignore Jesus, live a life of sin, and still go to Heaven (1 Corinthians 6:9-11)

- ◯ Believing I can hang around immoral people and not become corrupted in my thinking and actions (1 Corinthians 15:33-34)

- ◯ Believing I can escape the natural consequences of sin in this life (Galatians 6:7-8)

- ◯ Believing that I must gain the approval of certain people in order to be happy (Galatians 1:10)

- ◯ Believing that I must measure up to certain self-imposed goals in order to feel good about myself (Galatians 3:2-3; 5:1)

Use the following prayer of confession for each item above that you have believed. Pray through each item separately.

LET'S PRAY

Lord, I confess that I have been deceived by _____. I thank You for Your forgiveness, and I commit myself to only believing Your truth. Amen.

It is important to know that in addition to being deceived by the world, false teachers and deceiving spirits, you can also fool yourself. Now that you are alive in Christ, forgiven, and totally accepted, you don't need to live a lie or defend yourself like you used to. Christ is now your truth and defense.

WAYS YOU CAN DECEIVE YOURSELF:

- ◯ Learning what God expects (hearing God's Word) but not always doing it (James 1:22, 4:7)
- ◯ Saying that I have no sin in my life I need to be accountable for (1 John 1:8)
- ◯ Letting my pride inflate my ego and looking down on others (Galatians 6:3)
- ◯ Thinking that I can measure my wisdom by the world's standards (1 Corinthians 3:18-19)
- ◯ Thinking I can be a good Christian and still hurt others by what I say (James 1:22)
- ◯ Thinking my secret sin (such as lust, jealousy or hatred) will only hurt me but will not hurt others (Exodus 20:4-5)
- ◯ Thinking that I can have immoral friends and it will have no effect on me (1 Corinthians 15:33)
- ◯ Thinking that I can override God and get what I want by positive thinking or having some kind of special faith

Use the following prayer of confession for each item above that you have believed. Pray through each item separately.

LET'S PRAY

Lord, I confess that I have deceived myself by _____. I thank You for Your forgiveness and commit myself to believing Your truth.

WRONG WAYS OF DEFENDING YOURSELF:

- ○ Refusing to face the bad things that have happened to me (Denial of reality)
- ○ Escaping from the real world by daydreaming, binge watching, excessive computer or video game playing, music, plunging into social media, etc. (Fantasy and Distraction)
- ○ Withdrawing from people to avoid rejection (Emotional insulation)
- ○ Reverting (going back) to a less threatening time of life (Regression)
- ○ Taking out frustrations on others (Displaced anger)
- ○ Blaming others for my problems (Projection)
- ○ Making excuses for poor behavior (Rationalization)
- ○ Hypocrisy (trying to present a false image)

Use the following prayer of confession for each item above that you have participated in. Pray through each item separately.

LET'S PRAY

Lord, I confess that I have defended myself wrongly by _____.
I thank You for Your forgiveness and commit myself to trusting in You to defend and protect me.

Choosing the truth may be difficult if you have been living a lie and have been deceived for some time. The Christian needs only one defense: Jesus. Knowing that you are completely forgiven and accepted as God's child sets you free to face reality and declare your total dependence upon Him.

Faith is the biblical response to the truth, and believing the truth is a choice we can all make. If you say, "I want to believe God, but I just can't," you are being deceived. Of course, you can believe God because what God says is always true.

Faith is something you decide to do whether you feel like it or not. Believing the truth doesn't make it true; however, if something is true, **we are wise to simply believe it**.

The worldly wisdom twists the truth by teaching that we can create reality through what we believe. But the truth is we can't create accurate reality with our minds. Instead, we learn to distinguish and face reality with our minds. Simply "having faith" is not the key issue here. It's what or whom you believe that makes the difference. You see, everybody believes in something and everybody lives according to what he or she believes. The question is this: Is the object of your faith trustworthy? If what you believe isn't true, then how you live won't be right.

For centuries, Christians have known that it is important to tell others what they believe. Read aloud the following Statements of Truth, thinking about the words as you read them. Read it every day for several weeks. This will help renew your mind and replace any lies you have believed with the truth.

STATEMENTS OF TRUTH

1. I believe there is only one true and living God (Exodus 20:2-3) who is the Father, Son, and Holy Spirit. He is worthy of all honor, praise, and glory. I believe that He made all things and holds all things together (Colossians 1:16-17).

2. I recognize Jesus Christ as the Messiah, the Word who became flesh and lived with us (John 1:1, 14). I believe He came to destroy the works of Satan (1 John 3:8), and that He disarmed the rulers and authorities and made a public display of them having triumphed over them (Colossians 2:15).

3. I believe that God showed His love for me by having Jesus die for me, even though I was sinful (Romans 5:8). I believe that God rescued me from the dark power of Satan and brought me into the kingdom of His Son, who forgives my sins and sets me free (Colossians 1:13-14).

4. I believe I am spiritually strong because Jesus is my strength. I have authority to stand against Satan because I am God's child (1 John 3:1-3). I believe that I was saved by the grace of God through faith, that it was a gift and not the result of any works of mine (Ephesians 2:8-9).

5. I choose to be strong in the Lord and in the strength of His might (Ephesians 6:10). I put no confidence in the flesh (Philippians 3:3) because my weapons of spiritual battle are not of the flesh but are powerful through God for the tearing down of Satan's strongholds (2 Corinthians 10:4). I put on the whole armor of God (Ephesians 6:10-20), and I resolve to stand firm in my faith and resist the evil one (1 Peter 5:8-9).

6. I believe that apart from Christ I can do nothing (John 15:5), yet I can do all things through Him who strengthens me (Philippians 4:13). Therefore, I choose to rely totally on Christ. I choose to abide in Christ in order to bear much fruit and glorify the Lord (John 15:8). I announce to Satan that Jesus is my Lord (1 Corinthians 12:3), and I reject any counterfeit gifts or works of Satan in my life.

7. I believe that the truth will set me free (John 8:32). I stand against Satan's lies by taking every thought captive in obedience to Christ

(2 Corinthians 10:5). I believe that the Bible is the only reliable guide for my life (2 Timothy 3:15-16). I choose to speak the truth in love (Ephesians 4:15).

8. I choose to present my body as an instrument of righteousness, a living and holy sacrifice, and to renew my mind with God's Word (Romans 6:13; 12:1-2). I put off the old self with its evil practices and put on the new self (Colossians 3:9-10). I am a new creation in Christ (2 Corinthians 5:17).

9. I trust my Heavenly Father to direct my life and give me power to live by the Holy Spirit (Ephesians 5:18), so that He can guide me into all truth (John 16:13). I believe He will give me strength to live above sin and not carry out the desires of my flesh. I crucify the flesh, and I choose to be led by the Holy Spirit and obey Him (Galatians 5:16, 24).

10. I renounce all selfish goals and choose the greatest goal of love (1 Timothy 1:5). I choose to obey the two greatest commandments: to love the Lord my God with all my heart, soul, and mind and to love my neighbor as myself (Matthew 22:37-39).

11. I believe that Jesus has all authority in heaven and on earth (Matthew 28:18) and that He rules over everything (Colossians 2:10). I believe that Satan and his demons have been defeated by Christ and are subject to me since I am a member of Christ's Body (Ephesians 1:19-20; 2:6). I obey the command to submit to God and to resist the devil (James 4:7), and I command Satan, by the authority of the Lord Jesus Christ, to leave my presence.

STEP 3: BITTERNESS VS. FORGIVENESS

Let's start this step by acknowledging that by this point in your life, you've been hurt, maybe even deeply hurt. Maybe one particular person stands out to you or maybe it is a certain group of people you're thinking of right now. God didn't prevent this harm from coming to you. It is not surprising if those who hurt you are not fairly paying for their sin, neglect or treachery.

It has been said that holding grudges and harboring resentment is like swallowing a poison pill and hoping the person who hurt you dies. The Bible confirms that when you fail to forgive those who have hurt you, you become a wide-open target for Satan. God commands us to forgive others as we have been forgiven (Ephesians 4:32). You need to obey this command so that Satan can't take advantage of you (2 Corinthians 2:10-11). Christians are to forgive others and show them mercy because our Heavenly Father has shown us mercy (Luke 6:36). When you forgive like God forgives, you will experience release from the weight of bitterness in your soul, and healing will begin.

Nonetheless, this step can be very challenging for many people. If you have a heightened sense of nervousness, lean into the love of God. Remember, freedom comes when we move toward God by faith. Faith does not require you to first understand how forgiving those who hurt you brings healing and recovery. Faith just requires that you trust God enough to follow a process that allows you to transfer your hurt and desire for payback (justice) over to God. God alone is capable of absorbing your pain. God alone will hold everyone accountable for the pain they inflict on others. This step to freedom will guide you and maximize even the smallest amount of faith you have in this moment. So take courage. It's time to claim your freedom and healing. Let's do this!

There is a lot of confusion and incorrect teaching over biblical forgiveness. The following will help you to comprehend God's definition of forgiveness.

FORGIVENESS IS NOT FORGETTING. People who want to be able to forget all their pain before they get around to forgiving someone usually find they cannot. God commands us to forgive now. Confusion sometimes arises because Scripture says that God "will remember our sins no more" (Hebrews 10:17). But God knows everything and can't "forget" as if He had no memory of our sin. His promise is that He will never use our past against us (Psalm 103:10). The key issue is this: We may not be able to forget our past, but we can be free from it by forgiving others. When we bring up the past and use it against others, we are showing that we have not yet forgiven them (Mark 11:25).

FORGIVENESS IS A CHOICE, A DECISION OF THE WILL. SINCE GOD REQUIRES US TO FORGIVE, IT IS SOMETHING WE CAN DO. Forgiveness seems hard because it pulls against our sense of what is right and fair. We naturally want revenge for the things we have suffered. But we are told by God never to take our own revenge (Romans 12:19). You might be thinking, "Why should I let them off the hook?" And that is exactly the problem! As long as you do not forgive, you are still hooked to those who hurt you! You are still chained to your past. **By forgiving, you release those who hurt you from their debt to you, but they ultimately will still answer to God.** We must trust Him to deal with the other person justly, fairly, and mercifully, something we ourselves cannot do.

You might say, "But you don't know how much this person hurt me." However, until you let go of your hate and anger, he/she will continue to be able to hurt you. You stop the pain by forgiving him/her. **You forgive for your sake, so that you can be free. Forgiveness is really an issue of obedience between you and God. God wants you to be free; this is the only way.**

FORGIVENESS IS AGREEING TO LIVE WITH THE CONSEQUENCES OF ANOTHER PERSON'S SIN. Forgiveness costs you something. You choose to pay the price for the evil you forgive. That may seem horrible, but here is an important truth: **You will live with the consequences whether you want to or not. Your only choice is whether you will do so in the bondage of bitterness or in the freedom of forgiveness.** Of course, Jesus took the eternal consequences of all sin upon Himself. God "made Him who had no sin to be sin for us so that in Him we might become the righteousness of God" (2 Corinthians 5:21 NIV). However, we need to accept the temporary consequences of what was done to us. No one truly forgives without suffering the pain of another's sin. While that may seem unfair, justice is found at the cross, which makes forgiveness legally and morally right. As those who crucified Him mocked and jeered, Jesus prayed, "Father, forgive them for they do not know what they are doing" (Luke 23:34 NIV).

How do you forgive from your heart? You allow God to bring to the surface the mental agony, emotional pain and feelings of hurt towards those who hurt you. If your forgiveness does not reach down to the emotional core of your life, it will be incomplete. Too often we try to bury the pain inside us, making it hard to get in touch with how we really feel. Though we may not know how to or even want to bring our feelings to the surface, God does. Let God bring the pain to the surface so that He can deal with it. This is where God's gentle healing process begins.

FORGIVENESS IS THE DECISION NOT TO SEEK PERSONAL REVENGE OR ACTIVELY SHAME THOSE WHO HAVE WRONGED YOU. It is not unusual for us to remember a past, hurtful event and find anger and hate returning. It is tempting to bring up the issue with the one who hurt us in order to make him feel bad. But we must choose to take that thought of revenge captive to the obedience of Christ and choose to maintain forgiveness.

This doesn't mean that you must continue to put up with the future sins of others. God does not tolerate sin and neither should you. Nor should you put yourself in the position of being continually abused and hurt by the sins of others. You need to take a stand against sin while continuing to forgive those who hurt you. If you are trapped in an abusive situation, seek help from trusted authorities. Tell an adult who can make a difference. Call the police. It is also right and good to cooperate with authorities who seek to hold your abuser(s) accountable. God has appointed earthly authorities to enforce the law and defend those who have been harmed.

DON'T WAIT TO FORGIVE UNTIL YOU FEEL LIKE FORGIVING. You will never get there. Your emotions will begin to heal once you have obeyed God's command to forgive. Satan will have lost his power over you in that area, and God's healing touch will take over. **For now, it is freedom that will be gained, not necessarily a feeling.**

You can do this! Victory from your bondage and healing from your pain are yours today in Christ if you, by faith, obey God's instruction to forgive. So why wait? Begin this step by working through the following exercise.

Ask God to bring to your mind the names of those people you need to forgive by praying the following prayer out loud. (Remember to let this prayer come from your heart as well as your mouth!)

LET'S PRAY

Dear Heavenly Father, thanks for the kindness and patience you have with me. When I realize how good you are, it makes me want to be more like you and turn from my sins (Romans 2:4). I know I have not always been completely kind, patient and loving toward those who have hurt me. I have had bad thoughts and feelings toward these people. Today, I want to change that. I am asking You to bring to my mind all the people I need to forgive (Matthew 18:35). I ask You to bring to mind any painful memories associated with these people so I can choose to forgive them from my heart. I pray this in the precious name of Jesus who has forgiven me and who will heal me from my hurts. Amen.

Now, without stopping, go to the next page and list the names down the left side column that are coming to your mind right now.

NAME	WHAT THEY DID TO ME & THE TROUBLE IT HAS CAUSED IN MY LIFE	HOW IT MADE ME FEEL

After you've written all the names down that came to mind, return to the top and fill in the middle and right columns with information regarding each person you need to forgive. When you're finished, go to the next page.

Before continuing, it's important to consider two more names you may need to add to your list:

1. **Your own name.** You may blame yourself for consequences you've caused, or you've suffered from. If so, you might be tempted to think that it is noble for you to not forgive yourself. But that is exactly what Satan, the accuser, wants you to do. If you don't forgive yourself for the wrong you've done, you will be trapped in a mental pit of regret and self-pity. You will essentially keep a wall between you and God's love. To forgive yourself means to believe that God's grace is greater than your sin and mistakes. Though your sins may have darkly stained your soul, in Christ you are washed white as snow (Isaiah 1:18). When you are free from self-resentment, you can repair the damage you've done to others.

2. **God.** It may seem weird to forgive a person who is perfect and can absolutely do no wrong. But forgiving God doesn't mean that we are accusing Him of imperfection. Sometimes we hold disappointment and resentment against God because He did not shield us from harm, or He did not intervene in our trouble in the time-frame we expected him to act. Releasing bitterness, disappointment, and anger toward God by forgiving allows us to experience even deeper healing and true freedom. When we forgive, we open up our hearts to God and welcome the supernatural impact of God's restoration, love and blessing through faith in Christ.

Now you are ready to Biblically forgive and be set free from bitterness. You'll do this by using the prayers that are printed below. I realize that this might be the toughest thing God has ever asked you to do. Believe it; forgiving is the only way to be set free from the pain of the past. In Christ, you have the authority and power to complete this very important step. You can choose to forgive and finally be set free! Now is your time; don't let it pass you by.

As you pray, God may bring to mind painful memories that you had totally forgotten about. Let Him do this, even if it hurts. Connect with those strong emotions so that you can forgive from the heart.

Remember, forgiveness is dealing with your own pain and leaving the other person to deal with God. Good feelings will follow in time. Freeing yourself from the past is the critical issue right now.

Don't say, *"Lord, please help me to forgive."* He is already helping you and will be with you all the way through the process. Don't say, *"Lord, I want to forgive"* because it bypasses the hard choice we have to make. Say, **"Lord, I forgive."** As you move down your list, focus on each individual until you are sure you have dealt with all the remembered pain, everything the person did that hurt you, and how it made you feel (i.e. rejected, unloved, unworthy, dirty, etc.). Don't rush. Take as much time as you need. God will give you strength.

O.K., it's time to begin. Take each person on your list one at a time and pray aloud:

LET'S PRAY

Lord, I forgive _____(name the person)_____ for _____(say what he/she did to hurt you; be specific)_____, even though it made me feel _____(share the painful memories or feelings)_____.

Once you have dealt with every offense that has come to your mind and you have honestly expressed how that person hurt you, wrap up by praying the following for each individual on your list:

LET'S PRAY

Lord, I choose not to hold any of these things against _____(name)_____ any longer. I thank You for setting me free from the bondage of my bitterness toward him/her. I choose now to ask You to bless _____(name)_____. In Jesus' name, amen.

When you are finished, take the time to tear your forgiveness worksheet out of this workbook. Throw it away as a symbol of your decision to let go of the pain and trust God.

THE TRUTH ABOUT YOUR HEAVENLY FATHER

Before moving on to the next step, let's go a little deeper and think about how you've come to imagine God. Many Christians are not experiencing a close relationship or "connectedness" with their Heavenly Father because of lies they believe about God. This may be true for you as well. It's natural to project onto God the negative characteristics of authority figures who have hurt us. Now that you have made the choice to forgive those people, you may find your heart warming toward God in new ways.

Even though we are to have a healthy fear of God (awe of His holiness, power, and presence), as a follower of Jesus, we do not need to be afraid of God. Romans 8:15 (ESV), speaking of those who have put their faith and trust in Jesus Christ, says "for you did not receive the spirit of slavery to fall back into fear, but you have received the Spirit of adoption as sons, by whom we cry, 'Abba! Father!'" *(Note: "Abba" was an affectionate way for children to address their father during Bible times. It's the equivalent to "papa" or "daddy.")*

The following exercise will help break the chains of those lies and enable you to begin to experience that intimate "Abba, Father" relationship with Him. Work your way down this list, one-by-one, left to right. Begin each one with the statement at the top of that list. Read through the list aloud.

I RENOUNCE THE LIE THAT MY HEAVENLY FATHER IS...	I CHOOSE TO ACCEPT THE TRUTH THAT MY HEAVENLY FATHER IS...
1. distant and disinterested.	1. intimate and involved (Psalm 139:1-18).
2. insensitive and uncaring.	2. kind and compassionate (Psalm 103:8-14).
3. stern and demanding.	3. accepting and filled with joy and love (Romans 15:7; Zephaniah 3:17).
4. passive and cold.	4. warm and affectionate (Isaiah 40:11; Hosea 11:3-4).
5. absent or too busy for me.	5. always pleased with me and eager to spend time with me (Habakkuk 13:5; Jeremiah 31:20; Ezekiel 34:11-16).
6. never satisfied with what I do, impatient or angry.	6. patient, slow to anger, and pleased with me in Christ (Exodus 34:6; 2 Peter 3:9).
7. mean, cruel, or abusive.	7. loving, gentle, and protective of me (Jeremiah 31:3; Isaiah 42:3; Psalm 18:2).
8. trying to take all the fun out of life for me.	8. trustworthy. He wants to give me a full life. His will is good, perfect and acceptable (Lamentations 3:22-23; John 10:10; Romans 12:1-2).
9. controlling or manipulative.	9. full of grace and mercy, and He gives me freedom to fail (Hebrews 4:15-16; Luke 15:11-16).
10. condemning or unforgiving.	10. tenderhearted and forgiving. His heart and arms are always open to me (Psalm 130:1-4; Luke 15:17-24).
11. nit-picking, nagging or perfectionistic.	11. smiling as He thinks of me and proud of me as His growing child (Romans 8:28-29; Hebrews 12:5-11; 2 Corinthians 7:4).

I AM ONE OF GOD'S CHERISHED CHILDREN!
DEUTERONOMY 32:9-10

STEP 4: REBELLION VS. SUBMISSION

We live in rebellious times. Young people today often do not choose to respect people that God has placed in authority over them. You may have a problem living cooperatively under authority. You can easily be deceived into thinking that those in authority over you are robbing you of your freedom. In reality, however, God has established earthly authority for our protection.

At times, parents, teachers, bosses, pastors, coaches and other authority figures may abuse their position and treat us with disrespect or even abuse their authority in unkind and cruel ways. If this is the case, then the Bible encourages us to appeal and seek help from a higher authority for protection and justice. The laws where you live may require you to report the abuse you've experienced to the police or other protective agencies. If there is continuing abuse (physical, mental, emotional, or sexual), a higher-ranking authority can intervene and change the situation.

If someone in authority asks you to break God's law or compromise your sense of goodness, it is always best to obey God rather than men (Acts 5:29). But often, this is not the case.

In the modern world, there is a lot of money to be made from teen rebellion. Think about the movies, shows, fashion and music that target teen populations. It is also common to hear people talk about teen rebellion as a "phase" that everyone goes through. But the Bible clearly teaches that rebellion is not a phase that you eventually outgrow. Rebellion is a unique stronghold that rivals the power of witchcraft and the occult over a person's life (1 Samuel 15:23).

Here is another cruel fact about rebellion: when we run away from right authority, we always end up running into wrong authority. Gangs and human trafficking are just two examples of wicked systems that feed off of runaways and teens in rebellion. Rebellion is a fast track to bondage.

It is easy to believe the lie that those in right authority over us are only trying to rob us of the freedom to do what we want. The truth is, however, that God has placed them there for our protection and liberty. As a teen, your brain has not yet fully matured. Rebellion encourages young people to ignore the reality that they are not yet able to accurately measure risk and comprehend "cause and effect" in decision making.

Rebelling against God and rightful authorities is serious business because it gives Satan an opportunity to attack you. Submission is the only solution. God requires more of you, however, than just the outward appearance of cooperation. He wants you to sincerely submit to your authorities (especially parents) from the heart. When you understand the authority of those He has placed over you, you cut off this dangerous avenue of demonic attack.

The Bible makes it clear that we have two main responsibilities toward those in authority over us: pray for them and submit to them. Pray the following prayer out loud from your heart.

LET'S PRAY

Dear Heavenly Father, You have said in the Bible that rebellion is the same thing as witchcraft and being self-willed is like serving false gods (1 Samuel 15:23). I know that I have likely disobeyed and rebelled in my heart against You and those You have placed in authority over me. I thank You for Your forgiveness for my rebellion. By the shed blood of the Lord Jesus Christ, I pray that all doors that I have knowingly or unknowingly opened to evil spirits through my rebellion would now be closed. I pray that You will show me all the ways I have been rebellious. I now choose to adopt an obedient spirit and servant's heart. In Jesus' precious name, I pray. Amen.

Rebellion will often be expressed through an uncooperative attitude and a critical spirit. The following actions are signs of rebellion (or a rebellious attitude) in your heart. Check those that apply to the different authorities in your life.

- ○ Refusing to obey or follow legitimate instructions
- ○ Ignoring instructions or requirements, or adjusting them to suit myself
- ○ Believing it is my right to criticize those in authority over me
- ○ Making critical statements about authority figures
- ○ Rejecting the advice of others who have experience and wisdom
- ○ Finding fault easily with a person, group, or organization, particularly those in authority
- ○ Automatically assuming the worst when considering the things that others say or do
- ○ Passing along negative information to others who are not part of the problem or solution
- ○ Withdrawing from communicating with others (often shown by short, insensitive responses or silence)
- ○ Speaking disrespectfully to another person or about another person
- ○ Having to have the last words in a conversation

LET'S PRAY

Lord, I agree with You that I have been rebellious by _____.
Thank you for forgiving me for my rebellion.

We are all told to submit to one another as equals in Christ (Ephesians 5:21). In addition, however, God uses specific lines of authority to protect us and give order to our daily lives. Being under authority is an act of faith! And faith in God is greater in strength than our desire to exert our will and push back **against** authority. When we choose to comply with those in authority over us, we are demonstrating trust in God to work through His lines of authority for our good. Check each authority that you have been rebellious to.

- ○ Civil Government (including traffic laws, drinking laws, etc.) (Romans 13:1-7; 1 Peter 2:13-17)
- ○ Parents, step-parents or legal guardians (Ephesians 6:1-3)
- ○ Teachers, coaches and school officials (Romans 13:1-4)
- ○ Your boss (1 Peter 2:18-23)
- ○ Church Leaders (pastor, youth pastor, Sunday school teacher) (Hebrew 13:17)
- ○ God Himself (Daniel 9:5, 9)
- ○ House leaders, case workers, counselors (Romans 13:1-4)

Use the following prayer to ask the Lord to forgive you for those times you have been rebellious in attitude or actions.

LET'S PRAY

Lord, I agree with You that I have been rebellious toward ____(authority)____, by ____(action)____. Thank You for forgiving my rebellion. I choose to be submissive and to treat others with kindness and respect. In Jesus' name, amen.

REMEMBER

At times, parents, teachers, employers, and other authority figures may abuse their authority and break the laws which are ordained by God for the protection of innocent people. In those cases, you need to seek help from a *higher authority* for your protection. The laws in your area may require you to report such abuse to the police or other protective agencies. If there is continuing abuse (physical, mental, emotional, or sexual), at home or anywhere else, counseling may be needed to change the situation. If someone abuses their authority by asking you to break God's law or compromise yourself, you need to obey God rather than man (Acts 4:19-20).

STEP 5: PRIDE VS. HUMILITY

Pride is a killer. Pride says, "I can do it! I can get myself out of this mess without God or anyone else's help." Oh no, we can't! We absolutely need God, and we desperately need each other. Paul wrote that we "worship by the Spirit of God and glory in Christ Jesus and put no confidence in the flesh" (Philippians 3:3 ESV).

Humility is confidence properly placed in God. We are to be "strong in the Lord and in the strength of His might" (Ephesians 6:10 ESV). James 4:6-10 and 1 Peter 5:1-10 tell us that spiritual problems will follow when we are proud. Use the following prayer to express your commitment to live humbly before God:

LET'S PRAY

Dear Heavenly Father, You have said that pride goes before destruction and an arrogant spirit before stumbling (Proverbs 16:18). I confess that I have been thinking mainly of myself and not of others. I have not denied myself, picked up my cross daily and followed You (Matthew 16:24). And as a result, I have given ground to the enemy in my life. I have believed that I could be successful by living according to my own power and resources. Wonderful Father, help me to trust you more. Change my unbelief to belief.

I now confess that I have sinned against You by placing my will before Yours and by centering my life around myself instead of You. I renounce my pride and my selfishness and close any doors that I've opened in my life or physical body to the enemies of the Lord Jesus Christ. I choose to rely on the Holy Spirit's power and guidance so that I can do Your will.

I give my heart to You and stand against all of Satan's attacks. I ask you to show me how to live for others. I choose now to make others more important than myself and to make You the most important Person of all in my life (Rom. 12:10; Matt. 6:33). Please show me specifically now the ways in which I have lived pridefully. I ask this in the name of my Lord Jesus Christ. Amen.

Having made that commitment in prayer, now allow God to show you any specific areas of your life where you have been prideful, such as:

- ○ Having a stronger desire to do my will than God's
- ○ Relying on my own strength and abilities rather than on God's
- ○ Thinking my ideas are better than other people's
- ○ Wanting to control how others act rather than develop self-control
- ○ Considering myself more important than others
- ○ Having a tendency to think that I don't need people
- ○ Finding it difficult to admit when I am wrong
- ○ Being a people-pleaser rather than a God-pleaser
- ○ Being overly concerned about getting credit for doing good things
- ○ Thinking I am more humble than others
- ○ Thinking I am smarter than my parents/guardians
- ○ Feeling my needs are more important than other people's needs
- ○ Considering myself better than others because of my academic, artistic, or athletic abilities and accomplishments
- ○ Other

_____
_____
_____

For each of the above areas that has been true in your life, pray out loud:

LET'S PRAY

Lord, I agree I have been prideful in the area of _____. Thank You for forgiving me for this pridefulness. I choose to humble myself and place all my confidence in You. Amen.

Pride is the original sin. The devil is the original sinner. Many people think that Adam and Eve committed the first sin, but the Bible details a sinister plot that took place before God created Adam and Eve (Isaiah 14). The Devil, full of pride, tried to make a power move against God and dethrone the King and Creator of the universe. Of course, the Devil failed and sealed his fate. But this defeat did not produce humility and repentance. On the contrary, Satan's pride has continually plotted against God. Since the Devil is no match for God, he now turns his attention to those made in God's image: humanity. The Devil wants every human being to be full of pride. Why? Because pride disrupts human harmony and relational peace like nothing else. God wants us to be free from pride so that we can be peacemakers (Matthew 5:8) and bring humanity together rather than be divisive (2 Corinthians 5:19).

God's love is greater than pride. When God's people confess their pride and repent, the barriers that separate people begin to crumble. Carefully read the following verses:

> For Christ himself has brought peace to us. He united Jews and Gentiles into one people when, in his own body on the cross, he broke down the wall of hostility that separated us. He did this by ending the system of law with its commandments and regulations. He made peace between Jews and Gentiles by creating in himself one new people from the two groups. Together as one body, Christ reconciled both groups to God by means of his death on the cross, and our hostility toward each other was put to death.
> EPHESIANS 2:14-16 NLT

Racial prejudice, bigotry and hatred have long plagued the human the race. Many times, we deny that there is prejudice or bigotry in our hearts, yet as Hebrews says "nothing in all creation is hidden from God's sight. Everything is uncovered and laid bare before the eyes of him to whom we must give account" (Hebrews 4:13 NIV). The following is a prayer asking God to shine His light upon your heart and reveal any areas of prideful prejudice:

LET'S PRAY

Dear Heavenly Father, I know that You love all people equally and that You do not show favoritism, but You accept men from every nation who fear You and do what is right (Acts 10:34-35). You do not judge people based on skin color, race, ethnic background, gender, denominational preference or any other worldly matter (2 Corinthians 5:16). I confess that I have too often prejudged others or regarded myself as superior because of these things. I have not always been a servant of peace and respect but have been a proud agent of division through my attitudes, words and deeds. I repent of all hateful bigotry and prideful prejudice, and I ask You, Lord, to now reveal to my mind all the specific ways in which this form of pride has corrupted my heart and mind. In Jesus' name, Amen.

Check the following areas in which you have been prejudiced:

- ○ Thinking I am superior to another race of human beings or superior to another ethnic background (This could be racial, cultural or geographical. For example, it may include "city people", "country people", "southerners", etc.)
- ○ Thinking my gender is superior to the opposite
- ○ Thinking my life experience makes me superior to others
- ○ Thinking I am superior to my elders
- ○ Thinking I am more important than those younger than me
- ○ Thinking my practice of Christianity is more advanced than other Bible believing Christians
- ○ Looking down on others and being disrespectful toward people who do not yet understand the way of Jesus
- ○ Thinking I am superior to non-Christians because of my relationship with Christ and, therefore, failing to recognize that God's grace is unmerited
- ○ Other

_____
_____
_____
_____

For each of these areas, or others not listed that the Lord brings to mind, pray the following prayer aloud from your heart:

LET'S PRAY

I confess and renounce the prideful sin of prejudice against ___(name the group)___. I thank You for your forgiveness, Lord, and ask now that You would change my heart and make me a loving agent of peace and relational restoration with ___(name the group)___. In Jesus' name, Amen.

STEP 6: BONDAGE VS. FREEDOM

The next step to freedom deals with the sins that have become habits in your life. If you have been caught in the defeating cycle of "sin-confess-sin-confess," realize that full repentance is the key to spiritual victory. If we sin, we have the choice to confess our sin to God and then repent. We choose to turn away from our sin and instead focus our hearts and minds on God, surrendering to His rightful leadership over our lives. James 4:7 promises that when we submit to God in this way, the Devil will flee. Then, we will be able to successfully resist the temptation to sin in the same way again.

Habitual sin often requires help from spiritual leadership and a trusted brother or sister in Christ. James 5:16 says, "Confess your sins to each other and pray for each other so that you may be healed. The earnest prayer of a righteous person has great power and produces wonderful results" (NLT). The effective prayer of a righteous person can accomplish much." Reach out to a mature Christian authority figure (parent, pastor, teacher, counselor, etc.). Seek out a stronger Christian friend who will lift you up in prayer and care to keep you accountable in your areas of weakness.

Understand that the assurance of 1 John 1:9 is vital to victory: "If we confess our sins, He is faithful and just to forgive us our sins and to cleanse us from all unrighteousness" (ESV).

Remember, confession is not saying "I'm sorry"; it is openly admitting "I did it." Whether you need the help of others or just the accountability of God, pray the following prayer out loud:

LET'S PRAY

Dear Heavenly Father, You have told me to put on the Lord Jesus Christ and to not think about how to please my sinful desires (Romans 13:14). I confess that I have given in to sinful desires which wage war against my soul (1 Peter 2:11). I thank You that in Christ my sins are already forgiven, but I have broken Your holy law and given the devil a chance to wage war in my body (Romans 6:12-13; James 4:1; 1 Peter 5:8). I come to You now to confess and renounce these sins of the flesh (Proverbs 28:13; 2 Corinthians 4:2) so that I might be cleansed and set free from the bondage of sin. Please reveal to my mind now all the sins of the flesh I have committed and the ways I have grieved the Holy Spirit. In Jesus' name, I pray. Amen

There are many kinds of sins that can become habitual and eventually control us. The following list contains many of them. Carefully examine the following list and ask the Holy Spirit to reveal to your mind which ones from the past or the present you need to confess. Remember, He may bring to mind others that are not here. For each one that God reveals, pray the following prayer of confession from the heart:

NOTE: *Sexual sins, eating disorders, substance abuse, abortion, suicidal tendencies and perfectionism will be dealt with later in this step.*

- ○ stealing (including shop lifting and purposely not returning borrowed items to their rightful owners)
- ○ impure thoughts
- ○ lying/distorting the truth to get your way
- ○ eagerness for lustful pleasure
- ○ fighting
- ○ cheating
- ○ quarreling/arguing
- ○ gossip/slander
- ○ hatred
- ○ procrastination (irresponsibly putting things off)
- ○ jealousy, envy
- ○ swearing/cussing/vulgar joking
- ○ anger
- ○ greed/materialism
- ○ complaining and criticism
- ○ apathy/laziness
- ○ depression/hopelessness
- ○ Other

_____
_____
_____
_____
_____

LET'S PRAY

Lord, I admit that I have committed the sin of _____. I thank You for Your forgiveness and cleansing. I turn away from this sin and turn to You, Lord. Strengthen me by Your Holy Spirit to obey You. In Jesus' name. Amen.

"Sin" is an uncomfortable word that describes behavior against God's beautiful holiness. Sin cannot co-exist with God's holiness. God's holiness is described as a consuming fire that purifies and incinerates sin (Hebrews 12:29). The point is that God is perfect, and His universe will ultimately be restored to perfection, rightness and holiness. Sin, and sinners, face certain obliteration. But God, being rich in mercy, because of the great love with which He loves us, has set us free from the control of sin and delivered us from the certain judgment of sin through Jesus Christ (Ephesians 2:4-5; Romans 5:8). This is good news for all who believe in and surrender their lives to Jesus.

With this in mind, it is important to understand that true Christians are no longer sinners. Therefore, true Christians should not allow sin to guide our thoughts or rule our bodies. To do this, we must not use our bodies or another person's body as an instrument of unrighteousness

(Romans 6:12-13). Sexual sin is dangerous. It is not only a sin against God but a sin against body, soul and spirit (1 Corinthians 6:13-20). When we operate in a sexual manner outside of God's plan (holy marriage), we open ourselves to all manner of bondage including shame, confusion, an unresponsive conscience and so forth (Romans 1:18-32).

Sex has a purpose. It is designed by God and meant for human reproduction and for the loving and bonding pleasure between a husband and a wife. The Bible describes marital sex as a holy union that allows an adult man and an adult woman to be sacredly joined together body, soul and spirit. This holy sexual bonding is designed to help secure the sacred vows of a Christian wedding. The Devil does not want your generation to know and understand this truth.

Sexually connecting to another person (in whatever way) will create a bond. The question, therefore, becomes one of holiness. Marriage is a sacred pledge that produces holy attachment and bonding during sex. Instead of righteous bonding, sexual activity outside of marriage produces bondage in our souls. This may be hard to accept; nevertheless, it's true. Sexual immorality creates spiritual bondage whether it is heterosexual or homosexual, which is another important aspect to consider.

Nowhere in the Bible will you find God prohibiting love between individuals of the same sex/gender. In fact, some of the most notable relationships in the Bible highlight the love between same gender friends. However, sexual relations between people of the same sex are clearly forbidden by God. Why? Part of the reason God puts very specific rules around sex is that God intentionally designed sex to reflect the deeper love of spiritual oneness between Creator and humanity. This is a profound mystery (Ephesians 5: 31-32) that is better left for another day. But for now, you need to know that sexual sin is serious.

To find freedom from any sexual bondage that enslaves you, pray the following prayer:

LET'S PRAY

Dear Heavenly Father, I do not want any form of sexual sin to enslave me. Therefore, I ask you to bring to my mind every way that my body has engaged in sexual sin so that I can break all unholy bonding and ungodly attachment. In Jesus' name I pray. Amen.

Allow yourself to openly receive any memories and expressions of sex that are coming to mind. Please know that some of the sexual immorality you remember may have been forced on you (sexual assault, molestation, rape, incest, etc.). You will have the opportunity to break free from this type of bondage as well as unholy sexual acts that you willfully participated in or initiated (including pornography, lustful masturbation, lustful physical contact on any level with others, and virtual sex activities such as sexting, etc.). Make note of each of these experiences and engage your loving Heavenly Father with the following prayer:

LET'S PRAY

Dear Heavenly Father, I confess my sexual experience _____(name the sexual experience)_____ with _____(name the person or refer to the person if you don't remember their name)_____. I turn away from these experiences and behavior and gladly turn to You. I thank You for your forgiveness and cleansing from the sexual sin that has stained my soul. I ask You now to break the unholy bond with _____(name)_____ on every level-spiritually, emotionally and physically. I thank You for setting me free from this bondage. Amen.

Repeat this prayer for each memory and current involvement.

After you have completed this exercise, commit your body to God by praying out loud from your heart:

LET'S PRAY

Dear Father God, I renounce all these uses of my body in unholy ways and ask You to break all bondage Satan has brought into my life through my involvement. I admit my participation. Loving Father-God, I choose from this day forward to present my entire body to You as a channel of righteousness. I here and now consider my life a living expression of worship to You, holy and acceptable (Romans 12:1). I choose to reserve the sexual use of my body for holy marriage only (Hebrews 13:4).

I hereby reject the lie that my body is not clean or that it is dirty or in any way unacceptable to You or others as a result of my past sexual experiences. Father-God, I thank You that You have totally cleansed and forgiven me, and You love me without any hesitation. Therefore, I can accept myself and my body as cleansed in Your eyes. I thank you in Jesus' name. Amen.

SPECIAL PRAYERS FOR SPECIAL NEEDS

ABORTION

An important note: Just as mothers are called to be responsible for the life that God has entrusted to them, so, too, the father shares in this responsibility. If you have failed to fulfill your role as a parent and have been involved in the taking of an unborn life through abortion, pray the following prayer. This confession is an important part of a necessary grieving process that will open your heart and mind to the healing power of Jesus Christ.

Father-God, I confess that I was not a proper guardian and keeper of the life You entrusted to me, and I admit that as sin. I recognize my role in taking an unborn baby's life, and I ask for Your forgiveness. Thank You for Your forgiveness and cleansing. Because of your forgiveness, I now choose to forgive myself. In Jesus' name, I commit my unborn child to You for Your care for all eternity. Thank you for helping me to understand the preciousness of human life in the womb. From this day forward, I will respect the sacredness of unborn life. In Jesus' name. Amen.

PERFECTIONISM AND UNHEALTHY AMBITION

Father-God, I renounce the lie that my self-worth is dependent on my ability to perform and achieve. God, I confess that this lie causes me to constantly be concerned with what others think about me rather than rest in Your love and acceptance for me. I announce the truth that my identity and sense of worth is found in who I am as Your child. I renounce craving the approval and admiration of other people, and I choose to believe that I am already approved and cherished in Christ. Father-God, I choose to believe the truth that I have been saved, not by my ability to perform and achieve, but according to Your mercy and grace. I hereby reject the times that I have approached Christianity or religion as an opportunity to project perfection. I receive the free gift of eternal life in Christ and choose to rely on the Holy Spirit's power to make me more like Jesus every day. I renounce trying to be perfect by my own strength and will power. By your grace, Father-God, I choose from this day forward to walk by faith in the power of the Holy Spirit. In Jesus' name. Amen.

CONTROL

Father-God, many times people joke about "control freaks" but this is no laughing matter in my life. I confess that I have made a habit of self-soothing and regulating my negative emotions by overly ordering and requiring things to be my way. I have made a habit of imposing my will and exerting control over my personal world and relationships. This control, even when exerted in principled ways, has become a functional savior in my life that I have chosen to bow down to instead of You. I confess that my controlling attitude and behavior is a form of idolatry, and I repent of this practice. When I'm not in "control" and fret over not having my way, I miss out on the Holy Spirit's comfort and relief in my life (love, joy, peace, patience, kindness, faithfulness, gentleness and self-control; Galatians 5:22-23a). Even though I know how to get my way, I see now that it always comes at the expense of mistreating others and turning away from You. I choose now to surrender the details of my life to You Father-God. I ask You to forgive me for my stubbornness. I need Your daily help to trust You. Help me to learn to serve You with a glad heart even when things are not to my liking or preferences. Thank You for setting me free from this bondage. Please heal my soul from the pain that first produced this unhealthy coping and reveal to my mind any lies that I've believed as a result. In Jesus' name, amen.

EATING DISORDERS

Father-God, I confess that I have withheld food or ejected food from my body in ways that are not healthy but, instead, are harmful. I ask for Your forgiveness. I renounce the lie that my value as a person is dependent upon my physical appearance, my weight or size. I renounce vomiting, using laxatives, or starving myself as a means of control or cleansing myself of evil or altering my physical appearance. I announce that only the blood of the Lord Jesus Christ cleanses me from sin. I announce that in Christ I am accepted, secure and significant. I am loved just as I am by You, my Father-God. I now turn to You to meet my emotional needs.

FOR OVEREATING/OVERINDULGING:

Father-God, I confess that I have stuffed myself with food in harmful and unhealthy ways. I ask for Your forgiveness. I renounce the lie that an overfed stomach can sooth my soul and provide me with peace. Food has become an idol to me. I use it to regulate my emotions rather than turning to You, my God and Savior Jesus Christ. I confess my sin and choose now to repent and turn away from this harmful coping. I now turn to You to meet my emotional needs.

Continue the prayer by saying the following aloud:

When I choose to interfere with my rightful food intake, I miss out on the Holy Spirit's comfort and relief in my life (love, joy, peace, patience, kindness, faithfulness, gentleness and self-control; Galatians 5:22-23a). Even though interfering with my eating provides emotional results, I see now that it always comes at the expense of de-valuing my worth and turning away from You, my loving Father-God. I choose now to make my eating habits an expression of worship to you and faith in you. Even though I've formed a strong negative habit, Your power is greater, and my freedom is guaranteed in Christ. Help me to daily rest and trust in You. Help me to learn how to process my emotional disappointment and pain in healthy and positive ways. Thank You for setting me free from this bondage. Please heal my soul from that pain that first produced this unhealthy coping. In Jesus' name, Amen.

CUTTING/SELF-HARM

Father-God, I confess that I have willfully harmed and wounded my body, and I ask for your forgiveness. I renounce the lie that harming myself can release inner pain and bring peace to my soul. I renounce the lie that I can somehow rid myself of evil by inflicting myself with physical pain. I accept the reality that Jesus' body was broken on my behalf. His shed blood has, once and for all, delivered me from my sin. The wounding Jesus' flesh suffered as He was beaten and crucified secured my inner healing (Isaiah 53:4-5).

When I choose to harm myself in any way, I miss out on the Holy Spirit's comfort and relief in my life (love, joy, peace, patience, kindness, faithfulness, gentleness and self- control; Galatians 5:22-23a). Even though hurting myself provides immediate emotional impact, I see now that it always comes at the expense of de-valuing my worth and turning away from You, my loving Father-God. I choose now, from this point forward, to acknowledge that my body is united with my Savior, Jesus Christ (1 Corinthians 6:15). Jesus has already suffered in the flesh to deliver me from my inner pain. Therefore, I will not cause unnecessary harm to myself and to Jesus. I also acknowledge that my body is a temple of the Most High God (1 Corinthians 6: 19). Father-God, with Your help and power, from this point forward I will not deface, vandalize or disfigure my body. Help me to learn how to process my emotional pain in healthy and positive ways. Thank You for setting me free from this bondage. Please heal my soul from the pain that first produced this unhealthy coping. In Jesus' name, Amen.

GENDER IDENTITY AND HOMOSEXUALITY

Father-God, my gender identity and sexual orientation has been a point of confusion and, at times, embarrassment in my life. At times I haven't always felt like my soul belongs in the gender specific body it's been given. I also have experienced a strong desire to direct my sexuality toward those of the same sex. I now realize that You are the Creator God and You have designated gender distinctions since the beginning (Genesis 1:27). As the Creator God, You have also decreed that human beings maintain these distinctions between male and female bodies, and in Your infinite wisdom, You have forbidden same sex intimate relationships.

I confess that instead of seeking Your guidance in the Bible, I've been guilty of listening more to the wisdom of the world in this area of personal difficulty. Rather than accept my gender assignment from You, my Creator, I have sought out ways to express my will. I have also schemed to justify homosexual relationships. I ask for Your forgiveness. In order to be free and to honor Your complete plan of salvation, I must be willing to deny myself and pick up my cross (forsake that which seems natural to me) and follow Jesus. This principle is true not just for people in my situation, but also for anyone who wrestles with lifestyles that are not endorsed in Heaven. Therefore, Father-God, I renounce the lies that are meant to convince me that I am someone other than You created me to be. By the power of the Holy Spirit and the guidance of the Bible, I choose to accept my biological identity and to direct my sexuality in a way that reflects the principles in the Bible. I commit myself to the Scriptures so that my mind may be renewed in these areas. Father-God, guide me to wise counsel and comfort me in a way that heals the pain that made me vulnerable to the lies that have influenced my thinking and controlled my behavior in these areas.

Father-God, I hereby renounce all unbiblical thoughts, urges or drives that have distorted my relationships with others. I announce that I am free to embrace my God-given gender and to relate to the opposite sex and my own sex in the way that You intended. I pray all of this in the precious name of Jesus. Amen.

SUBSTANCE ABUSE

Father-God, I confess that I have abused and misused substances (alcohol, tobacco, prescription or street drugs) for the purpose of pleasure, to escape reality, or to cope with difficult problems. In doing so, I confess that I have abused my body and impacted my brain in a harmful way. I ask for Your forgiveness.

When I choose to abuse and misuse substances, I miss out on the Holy Spirit's comfort and relief in my life (love, joy, peace, patience, kindness, faithfulness, gentleness and self- control; Galatians 5:22-23a). Even though these substances provide immediate emotional impact, I see now that it always comes at the expense of altering my brain chemistry and turning away from You, my loving Father-God. I choose now, from this point forward, to acknowledge that my body is united with my Savior Jesus Christ (1 Corinthians 6:15). Therefore, I will not alter my sobriety and cause unnecessary distortion in my loving connection with Jesus. I also acknowledge that my brain is the control center where I make personal choices in ways that are godly or ungodly. I choose this day to be sober minded so that I can choose to do right and no longer be vulnerable to the Devil's tactics and temptation (1 Peter 5: 8). I also acknowledge that my body is a temple of the Most High God (1 Corinthians 6: 19). With Your help and power, God, from this point forward, I will not consume any illegal substance. I will wait until I am legally old enough to prayerfully consider controlled substances like alcohol and tobacco products. Help me to learn how to process my emotional pain in healthy and positive ways. Thank You for setting me free from this bondage. Please heal my soul from the pain that first produced this unhealthy coping. In Jesus' name, Amen.

SUICIDAL TENDENCIES

Lord, I confess that I have entertained suicidal thoughts and/or plotted to end my life. I ask for your forgiveness. I renounce all suicidal thoughts along with any threats and attempts I have made to take my own life. I renounce the lie that life is hopeless and that I can find peace and freedom by ending my own life. I also acknowledge that to threaten suicide as a way of making a point is equally dangerous since the threat stems from unevaluated emotions, and it has the power to become lodged in my thinking as an option or even a secret vow. I declare that Satan is the father of lies and comes to steal, kill and destroy. I choose to believe that no earthly circumstance, person or power can stand in the way of God's plan for my life. I embrace the assurance of God's Word that God's plan for me is perfect and ultimately designed to bring about the best in God's will. I choose to believe Jesus when He promised to give me life and to give it to the full (John 10:10). I choose to accept Your forgiveness and to believe that there is always hope in Christ. In Jesus' name. Amen.

After you have utilized these special prayers, conclude by saying loud the following from the heart:

LET'S PRAY

Father-God, after confessing these sins to You, I claim through the blood of the Lord Jesus Christ my forgiveness and cleansing. I cancel all ground that evil spirits have gained through my willful involvement in sin. I ask this in the wonderful name of my Lord and Savior, Jesus Christ. Amen!

FREEDOM FROM FEAR

If you are struggling to walk by faith, it may be because of fears that curse your life. To gain freedom and walk in victory, you will need to address any dominating fears by the authority and power of Jesus Christ. The Bible declares that our enemy, the devil, prowls around like a roaring lion, seeking people to devour (1 Peter 5:8). Just as a lion's roar strikes terror in the hearts of those who hear it, so Satan uses fear to try to paralyze Christians. His intimidation tactics are designed to rob us of faith in God and drive us to try to get our needs met by irrational means.

Fear weakens us, causes us to be self-centered, and clouds our minds so that all we can think about is the thing that frightens us. But fear can only control us if we let it.

God, however, does not want us to be mastered by anything, including fear (1 Corinthians 6:12). Jesus Christ is to be our only Master (2 Timothy 2:21; John 13:13). In order to begin to experience freedom from the bondage of fear and be able to walk in the power of the Holy Spirit, pray the following prayer from your heart:

LET'S PRAY

Dear Heavenly Father, I confess to you that I have listened to the devil's roar and have allowed fear to master me. I have not always walked by faith in You but instead have focused on my feelings and circumstances (2 Corinthians 4:16-18; 5:7). I ask You to forgive me for my unbelief. Right now, I renounce the spirit of fear and affirm the truth that You have not given me a spirit of fear but of **power**, **love** and a **sound mind** (2 Timothy 1:7). Lord, please reveal to my mind now all the fears that have been controlling me so that I can renounce them and be free to walk by faith in You. I thank You for the freedom You give me to walk by faith and not by fear. In Jesus' powerful name I pray. Amen.

The following list may help you to recognize some of the fears that the devil has used to keep you from walking by faith. Check the ones that apply to your life. Write down any others that the Spirit of God brings to your mind. Then, one by one, renounce those fears aloud, using the suggested renunciation on the following page.

- ○ Fear of death
- ○ Fear of being a hopeless case
- ○ Fear of Satan and demons
- ○ Fear of losing my salvation
- ○ Fear of failure
- ○ Fear of having committed the unpardonable sin
- ○ Fear of rejection by people
- ○ Fear of disapproval
- ○ Fear of not being loved by God
- ○ Fear of poverty
- ○ Fear of embarrassment and shame
- ○ Fear of never getting married or being able to love or be loved by anyone
- ○ Fear of being victimized by crime
- ○ Fear of becoming homosexual
- ○ Fear of marriage
- ○ Fear of the death of a loved one
- ○ Fear of divorce
- ○ Fear of losing my mind
- ○ Fear of pain, injury and disease
- ○ Fear of the future/fear of change
- ○ Fear of specific people
- ○ Other specific fears that come to mind

_____
_____
_____
_____
_____

LET'S PRAY

I renounce the fear of _____ because God has not given me a spirit of fear. I choose to live by faith in God who has promised to protect me and meet all my needs as I walk by faith in Him (Psalm 27:1; Matthew 6:33-34).

After you have finished renouncing all the specific fears that you have allowed to control you, pray the following prayer from your heart:

LET'S PRAY

Dear Heavenly Father, I thank You that You are trustworthy. I choose to believe You even when my feelings and circumstances tell me to fear. You have told me not to fear, for You are with me; not to anxiously look about, for You are my God. You will strengthen me, help me, and surely uphold me with Your righteous right hand (Isaiah 41:10). I pray this with faith in the name of Jesus, my Savior, Loving Master and Friend. Amen.

ANALYZING YOUR FEAR

In order not to fall back into patterns of unhealthy fear, it's helpful to think carefully about the following: *When did you first experience the fear, and what events led up to that first experience? What lies have you believed that are the basis for the fear? How has the fear kept you from living for Jesus or compromised your testimony to others?*

Now that you have confessed your fears and have been set free from the bondage of fear, work out a plan of responsible behavior and determine ahead of time how you will respond when you encounter a fear object. You may need the help of a trusted adult, pastor or Christian professional to help you think through this process. Commit yourself to make and follow through with a personalized plan. Choosing to trust in God's protection when you are exposed to the things you once feared will build your faith and kill any fear that tries to overcome you.

STEP 7: CURSES VS. BLESSINGS

The last step to freedom is to renounce the sins of your ancestors and any curses which may have been placed on you directly or indirectly by family members, extended family members and/or biological parents. Many people don't realize this, but when God gave mankind the Ten Commandments for guidance, He revealed that sin has the power to attach to multiple generations in a family (Exodus 20:4-6). Christians have historically referred to this as "generational curses." You might have heard it referred to as "family dysfunction."

It's true that family chaos, dysfunction or sin can be passed from one generation to the next. Demonic spirits take advantage of this reality and enslave certain families in undeniable ways. This bondage can remain in place even with the most sincere Christian if he or she does not recognize and renounce generational sins and curses.

It's important to understand that this final step to freedom in Christ does not require you to renounce your family members or loved ones. But it does require you to specifically name the sins and wrongful habits your family and ancestors have been characterized by. In doing so, you will be free to claim your new spiritual heritage in Christ! Again, *you are not guilty for the sin of your ancestors*, but because of their sin, the devil may have gained leverage over your family's way of thinking and behaving.

Some examples of generational sins/curses are as follows:

- stealing (including shop lifting and purposely not returning borrowed items to their rightful owners)
- lying/distorting the truth to get your way
- eagerness for lustful pleasure
- fighting
- cheating
- quarreling/arguing
- gossip/slander
- hatred
- prejudice/bigotry/racism
- procrastination (irresponsibly putting things off)
- jealousy/envy
- swearing/cussing/vulgar joking
- anger
- greed/materialism
- complaining and criticism
- apathy/laziness
- depression/hopelessness
- ignoring or refusing to address uncomfortable situations or alarming behavior in family members
- holding grudges/bitterness/unforgiveness
- other _____
  _____

You probably recognize these sins from the list you personally addressed in Step 6. In this step, we are going to let the Lord Jesus break any bondage that came about through your ancestors and family.

Ask the Lord to show you specifically what sins are characteristic of your family by praying the following prayer. Then list those sins in the space provided below.

LET'S PRAY

Dear Heavenly Father, I ask You to reveal to my mind all the sins of my ancestors that are being passed down through family lines. I want to be free from those influences and walk in my new identity as a child of God. Amen.

As the Lord brings those areas of family sins to your mind, list them below. You will be renouncing them specifically later in this step.

1. _____
2. _____
3. _____
4. _____
5. _____
6. _____

In addition, deceived and evil people may have spoken curses over you. Satanic groups may have targeted you. No matter. You have all the authority and protection you need in Christ to stand against such curses.

In order to walk free from the sins of your ancestors and any demonic influences, read the following declaration and pray the following prayer out loud. Let the words come from your heart as you remember the authority you have in Christ Jesus.

DECLARATION

I here and now reject and disown all the sins of my ancestors. I specifically renounce the sins of _____(mention each specific sin out loud)_____. As one who has now been delivered from the domain of darkness into the kingdom of God's Son, I cancel out all sin and demonic working that has been passed down to me from my family. As one who has been redeemed by God and eternally united with Jesus Christ, I renounce all satanic strategies and assignments that are directed toward me and my ministry. I cancel out every curse that Satan and his workers have put on me. I announce to Satan and all his forces that Christ became a curse for me when He died for my sins on the cross (Gal. 3:13). I reject any and every way in which Satan may try to claim ownership of me. I belong to the Lord Jesus Christ who purchased me with His own blood. I reject any Satanic sacrifices or curses that unknowingly have been conducted toward me. In Jesus' name I rightly declare Jesus as Lord and renounce any claim that Satan may falsely make over me. I declare myself to be fully and eternally signed over and committed to the Lord Jesus Christ. By the authority I have in Christ, I now command every evil spirit and every enemy of the Lord Jesus that has been influencing me to leave my presence. I commit myself to my heavenly Father to do His will from this day forward.

LET'S PRAY

Dear Heavenly Father, I come to you as Your grateful child, bought out of slavery to sin by the blood of the Lord Jesus Christ. You are the Lord of all creation and the Lord of my life. I submit my body to You as an instrument of righteousness, a living and holy sacrifice, that I may glorify You in my body. I now ask You to fill me with the Holy Spirit. I commit myself to the renewing of my mind in order to prove that Your will is good, acceptable and perfect for me. All this I pray in the name and authority of the risen Lord Jesus Christ. Amen.

MAINTAINING YOUR FREEDOM

Congratulations! Now that you have gone through these seven steps, you may find old habits or temptations attempt to regain control of your mind in the days and weeks ahead. Therefore, it's important that you understand that the Christian victory and freedom cannot be obtained by being idle with your faith. You will need to understand how to maintain the freedom you have now gained. One person shared that she heard a spirit say to her mind "I'm back" two days after she had been set free. "No, you're not!" she proclaimed aloud. The attack stopped immediately.

The devil is attracted to sin like flies are attracted to garbage. Get rid of the garbage and the flies will depart for smellier places. In other words, if you walk in the truth, quickly confess all sin and forgive those who hurt you, then the devil will have no place in your life to set up shop. Even though sinless perfection is not something a mortal human can master in this life, you can walk blamelessly before God. Think of the following promise in the Bible as your soul's **disinfectant** and **sanitizer**:

> If we confess our sins, He is faithful and just to forgive us our sins and to cleanse us from all unrighteousness
> 1 JOHN 1:9 ESV

Realize that one victory does not mean the battles are over. After completing *The Steps*, one cheerful teen asked, "Will I always be like this?" I told her that she would stay free as long as she remained in an honest relationship with God. "Even if you slip and fall," I encouraged, "you know how to get right with God again."

One victim of incredible abuse shared this illustration: "It's like being forced to play a game with an ugly stranger in my own home. I kept losing and wanted to quit, but the ugly stranger wouldn't let me. Finally, I called for help. Jesus showed up and threw the stranger out. The ugly stranger knocked on the door trying to regain entry, but this time I recognized his voice and didn't let him in."

What a beautiful illustration of gaining freedom in Christ. We call upon Jesus, the final and most powerful authority, and He kicks the powers of darkness out of our lives.

Maintaining your freedom will require that you keep your eyes wide open for the devil's schemes and trickery. You must learn to utilize God's strategy for victory:

> **Submit yourselves therefore to God. Resist the devil, and he will flee from you.**
> JAMES 4:7 ESV

For the follower of Jesus, the question is never "Am I facing battle today?" Instead, the question we must ask is **"Am I *winning* the battle today?"**

Genuine life transformation is the result of a renewed mind (Romans 12:2). Therefore, you will most likely benefit from additional counseling with a trusted adult who is familiar with *The Steps to Freedom in Christ*.

REMEMBER: FREEDOM MUST BE MAINTAINED!

We cannot emphasize this point enough. By God's grace, you have won a very important battle in an ongoing war. Freedom will remain yours as long as you keep choosing truth and standing firm in the strength of the Lord. If new memories should surface, if you become aware of "lies" that you hadn't realized before, or if you remember or are exposed to other non-Christian experiences, then renounce them and choose the truth. If you realize that there are some other people you still need to forgive, Step 3 will remind you what to do. Most people have found it helpful to walk through *The Steps to Freedom in Christ* again and again as needed to resolve spiritual and personal conflict. If you do, be sure to take your time and read the instructions carefully.

We recommend that you read the book, *Stomping Out the Darkness*, to strengthen your understanding of your identity in Christ. *The Bondage Breaker Youth Edition* will help you overcome spiritual problems. You may also want to check out some of our other resources for freedom and spiritual growth on the Freedom in Christ Bookstore website: www.freedominchrist.com.

TO KEEP THE MOMENTUM OF YOUR FREEDOM GOING STRONG, WE ALSO SUGGEST THE FOLLOWING PRIORITIES:

- Get involved in a loving church youth group or Bible study where you can be open and honest with other believers your age.
- Study your Bible daily. There are many great youth Bibles around for you to use. Begin to get into God's Word and memorize key verses. Remember *it is the truth that sets you free and it is the truth that keeps you free!*
- Take the 30-day challenge! Commit to saying the "Who I am in Christ" statements out loud daily and study the verses for the next 30 days.
- Pay attention to what you're thinking about! Learn to take every thought captive to the obedience of Christ. Assume responsibility for your thought life. Don't let your mind go passive. Reject all lies, choose to focus on the truth, and stand firm in your identity in Christ.
- Don't drift away! It is very easy to become lazy in your thoughts and slip back into old habit patterns of thinking. Share your struggles openly with a trusted friend who will pray for you.
- Don't expect others to fight your battles for you. They can't, and they won't. Others can encourage you, but they can't think, pray, read the Bible or choose the truth for you.
- You can pray the suggested prayers in the Appendix often and with confidence.

For Special prayers for every day, bedtime, and cleansing home, apartment, or room, go to **Appendix C**.

Continue to seek your identity and sense of worth through who you are in Christ. Renew your mind with the truth that your *acceptance, security* and *significance* are in Christ alone. Meditate on the following truths daily, reading the entire list out loud, morning and evening, over the next few weeks.

IN CHRIST

I AM ACCEPTED

I am a child of God. (John 1:12)

I am Jesus' chosen friend. (John 15:15)

I am holy and acceptable to God (justified). (Rom. 5:1)

I am united to the Lord and am one spirit with Him. (1 Corinthians 3:16)

I have been bought with a price. I belong to God. (1 Corinthians 6:19, 20)

I am a part of Christ's body, a part of his family. (1 Corinthians 12:27)

I am a saint, a holy one. (Ephesians 1:1)

I have been adopted as God's child. (Ephesians 1:5)

I have been bought back (redeemed) and forgiven of all my sins. (Colossians 1:14)

I am complete in Christ. (Colossians 2:10)

I AM SECURE

I am free forever from punishment. (Romans 8:1- 2)

I am sure all things work together for good. (Romans 8:28)

I am free from any condemning charges against me. (Romans 8:31f)

I cannot be separated from the love of God. (Romans 8:35f)

I am hidden with Christ in God. (Colossians 3:3)

I am sure that the good work that God has started in me will be finished. (Philippians 1:6)

I am a citizen of heaven with the rest of God's family. (Ephesians 2:19)

I can find grace and mercy in times of need. (Hebrews 4:16)

I am born of God and the evil one cannot touch me. (1 John 5:18)

I AM SIGNIFICANT

I am salt and light for everyone around me. (Matthew 5:13,14)

I am part of the true vine, joined to Christ and able to produce lots of fruit. (John 15:1, 5)

I am hand-picked by Jesus to bear fruit. (John 15:16)

I am a Spirit-empowered witness of Christ. (Acts 1:8)

I am a temple where the Holy Spirit lives. (1 Corinthians 3:16; 6:19)

I am at peace with God and He has given me the work of
making peace between Himself and other people. (2 Corinthians 5:17f.)

I am God's co-worker. (2 Corinthians 6:1)

I am seated with Christ in heaven. (Ephesians 2:6)

I am God's building project, His handiwork, created to do His work. (Ephesians 2:10)

I am able to do all things through Christ who gives me strength! (Philippians 4:13)

APPENDIX A

PREPARATION FOR TAKING SOMEONE THROUGH *THE STEPS TO FREEDOM IN CHRIST*

Before you start *The Steps to Freedom in Christ*, go over the events of your life so that you understand the areas that might need to be dealt with. If you have the Confidential Personal Inventory (CPI), it would be helpful to fill it out now.

FAMILY HISTORY:

- Religious background of parents and grandparents
- Your home life from childhood to the present
- Any history of physical or emotional problems in the family
- Adoption, foster care, guardians

PERSONAL HISTORY:

- **Spiritual journey:** Do you know if you are saved? (If yes) How do you know you are saved? When did that happen?

- **Eating habits:** Do you make yourself vomit, take laxatives, or starve yourself to lose weight? Do you binge or eat uncontrollably?

- **Self-Harm:** Have you ever purposely scarred or caused injury to your body?

- **Free time:**
    - How many hours of TV do you watch a day?
    - What are your favorite TV shows?
    - How much time do you spend playing video/computer games each day?
    - How much time do you spend listening to music a day?
    - What kind of music do you listen to?
    - How much time do you spend reading each day?
    - What do you spend most of your time reading?
    - Do you smoke? Chew tobacco? Drink alcohol?
    - Do you use street drugs? If so, what kind?
    - Prescription drugs? What for?
    - Have you ever run away from home?
    - Do you have trouble sleeping too little or too much?
    - Frequent or recurring nightmares?
    - Were you ever raped or abused sexually, physically, verbally, or emotionally?
    - Do you suffer from distracting thoughts while in church, prayer, or Bible study?

PHYSICAL LIFE: (Check those that apply)

- ○ frequent headaches/migraines
- ○ memory problems
- ○ constant tiredness
- ○ fainting spells/dizziness
- ○ stomach problems
- ○ allergies

THOUGHT LIFE: (Check those that apply)

- ○ day dreaming/fantasy
- ○ insecurity
- ○ thoughts of inferiority
- ○ worry
- ○ thoughts of inadequacy
- ○ self-hate thoughts
- ○ perfectionism
- ○ doubts about salvation or God's love
- ○ lust
- ○ thoughts of suicide

EMOTIONAL LIFE: (Check those that apply)

- ○ feelings of frustration
- ○ fear of death
- ○ anger
- ○ fear of losing your mind
- ○ anxiety
- ○ fear of confusion
- ○ depression
- ○ fear of failure
- ○ guilt
- ○ fear of going to hell
- ○ loneliness
- ○ fear of the dark
- ○ worthlessness
- ○ fear of parents divorcing
- ○ bitterness

APPENDIX B

SATANIC RITUAL ABUSE RENUNCIATIONS

If you have been involved in any satanic rituals or heavy occult activity, you need to say aloud the following special renunciations and affirmations.

Read across the page, renouncing the first item in the column under "Kingdom of Darkness," and then affirming the first truth in the column under "Kingdom of Light." Continue down the entire list in that manner.

KINGDOM OF DARKNESS	KINGDOM OF LIGHT
1. I renounce ever signing my name over to Satan or having my name signed over to Satan by someone else.	1. I announce that my name is now written in the Lamb's Book of Life.
2. I renounce any ceremony where I was wed to Satan.	2. I announce that I am the Bride of Christ.
3. I renounce any and all covenants, agreements, or promises that I made with Satan.	3. I announce that I am in a new covenant with Jesus Christ alone.
4. I renounce all satanic assignments for my life, including duties, marriage and children.	4. I announce and commit myself to know and do only the will of God, and I accept only His guidance for my life.
5. I renounce all spirit guides assigned to me.	5. I announce and accept only the leading of the Holy Spirit.
6. I renounce ever giving of my blood in the service of Satan.	6. I trust only in the shed blood of my Lord Jesus Christ.
7. I renounce ever eating flesh or drinking blood in satanic worship.	7. By faith, I partake in Communion which represents the flesh and the blood of the Lord Jesus.
8. I renounce all guardians and satanic parents that were assigned to me.	8. I announce that God is my Heavenly Father, and the Holy Spirit is my guardian by whom I am sealed.
9. I renounce any baptism whereby I am identified with Satan.	9. I announce that I have been baptized into Christ Jesus and my identity is now in Him.
10. I renounce every sacrifice made on my behalf by which Satan may claim ownership of me.	10. I announce that only the sacrifice of Christ has any claim on me. I belong to Him. I have been purchased by the blood of the Lamb.

All satanic rituals, covenants (promises), and assignments must be specifically renounced as the Lord brings them to your mind. Some people who have been subjected to Satanic Ritual Abuse (SRA) develop multiple personalities (alters) in order to cope with their pain. In this case, you need someone who understands spiritual conflicts to help you maintain control and not be deceived into false memories. You can continue to walk through *The Steps to Freedom in Christ* to resolve all that you are aware of. Only Jesus can bind up the broken-hearted, set captives free, and make us whole.

APPENDIX C

DAILY PRAYER, BEDTIME PRAYER, & PRAYER FOR CLEANSING HOME/APARTMENT/ROOM

DAILY PRAYER

Dear Heavenly Father, I honor You as my Lord. I know that You are always present with me. You are the only all-powerful and only-wise God. You are kind and loving in all Your ways. I love You and I thank You that I am united with Christ and spiritually alive in Him. I choose not to love the world, and I crucify the flesh and all its passions.

I thank You for the life that I now have in Christ, and I ask You to fill me and guide me with Your Holy Spirit so I may live my life free from sin. I declare my dependence upon You, and I take my stand against Satan and all his lying ways. I choose to believe the truth, and I refuse to be discouraged. You are the God of all hope and I am confident that You will meet my needs as I seek to live according to Your Word. I express with confidence that I can live a responsible life through Christ Who strengthens me.

I now take my stand against Satan and command him and all his evil spirits to depart from me. I put on the whole armor of God. I submit my body as a living sacrifice and renew my mind by the living Word of God in order that I may prove that the will of God is good, acceptable and perfect. I ask these things in the powerful and precious name of my Lord and Savior, Jesus Christ. Amen.

BEDTIME PRAYER

Thank you, Lord, that you have brought me into Your family and have blessed me with every spiritual blessing in the heavenly realms in Christ. Thank you, too, for providing this time of renewal through sleep. I accept it as part of Your perfect plan for Your children, and I trust You to guard my mind and my body during sleep. As I have thought about You and Your truth during the day, I choose to let those thoughts continue in my mind while I am asleep. I commit myself to You for Your protection from every attempt of Satan or his demons to attack me during the night. I commit myself to You as my rock, my fortress, and my resting place. I pray in the strong name of the Lord Jesus Christ. Amen.

CLEANSING HOME/APARTMENT/ROOM

After destroying all articles of false worship (crystals, good luck charms, occultic objects, games, etc.) from your room, pray out loud in your sleeping area:

Thank you, Heavenly Father, for a place to live and be renewed by sleep. I ask You to set aside my room (or portion of room) as a place of safety for me. I renounce any worship given to false gods or spirits by other occupants, and I renounce any claim to this room (space) by Satan, based on what people have done here or what I have done in the past.

On the basis of my position as a child of God and a joint heir with Christ Who has all authority in heaven and on earth, I command all evil spirits to leave this place and never to return. I ask You, Heavenly Father, to appoint guardian angels to protect me while I live here. I pray this in the name of the Lord Jesus Christ. Amen.

www.ingramcontent.com/pod-product-compliance
Lightning Source LLC
Chambersburg PA
CBHW060427010526
44118CB00017B/2399